GWEN JOHN & CELIA PAUL

Painters in Parallel

Text and poem by Rowan Williams

Published to coincide with the exhibitions:

'GWEN JOHN AND CELIA PAUL: PAINTERS IN PARALLEL'
6 October 2012 – 3 February 2013 at Pallant House Gallery

'CELIA PAUL: SEPARATION'
6 October – 20 November 2012 in Chichester Cathedral

Catalogue published by Marlborough Fine Art

Pallant House Gallery
9 North Pallant
Chichester
West Sussex
PO19 1TJ

www.pallant.org.uk
Tel: 01243 774 557

GWEN JOHN IN PARIS
for Celia

I

I am Mrs Noah: my clothes-peg head
pins sheets out between showers;
in my clean cabin, my neat bed,
the bearded Augusti lumber in and out.

I am Mrs Noah: I call the beasts home
together, the cat to lie down with the slug,
the nun with the flapper. I comb
The hair of ferns to dry on deck.

I am Mrs Noah: arranging the flowers
in bright dust round my garden shed,
I watch the silent sky without doubt,
in the soaked moonlit grass sleep without dread.

I am Mrs Noah: the blossoms in the jug
throw their dense pollen round the stormy room like foam:
my hands hold beasts and friends and light in check
shaping their own thick gauzy rainbow dome.

II

Rodin's fingers: probe, pinch, ease open,
polish, calm. Keep still, he says,
recueille-toi: sit on the rock,
gaze out to sea, and I shall make you
patience on a monument. Keep still.
I kept still: he looked away.

On the stairs. In the yard. I stood,
not noticed, in the middle of half-broken stone,
aborted figures. I was a failed work,
keeping still among the darting birds.
His hand refused to close, my lips
stayed open all hours. He might drop in.

Brushing against Rilke in the corridor:
He smiles with fear or pity. Angels,
polished and black, bump into us
at strange angles. Afternoon light
swells like a thundercloud in the attic, busy
around an empty chair, draped like the dead king's throne.

III [1]

Thérèse dreamed her father
stood with his head wrapped
in black, lost.

Thérèse looks at the photographer
under his cloth and sees
Papa not seeing her.

I watch Thérèse watching
Papa and wondering when
the cloth comes off.

I watch her thinking
you can spend a short life
not being seen.

Thérèse looks at me and says,
Only when you can't see him do you
know you're there.

She says, Can you see me
not seeing you? That's when
you see me.

IV

I sent the boys off with their father.
I shall wait on the drenched hill,
Meudon, my Ararat, where the colours pour
into the lines of a leaf's twist.

And the backs of the chairs and schoolgirls' plaits at Mass
are the drawn discord, expecting
the absolution of light in the last bar.

Dr Rowan Williams
Archbishop of Canterbury

First published in the *Poems of Rowan Williams*,
Perpetua Press, Oxford, 2002.

1 Gwen John made numerous sketches of photographs
   of St Thérèse of Lisieux as a child.

A Corner of the Artist's Room in Paris 1907–1909

Oil on canvas
31.7 × 26.7 cm
Presented, May 1964, Museums Sheffield

GWEN JOHN/CELIA PAUL

Dr Rowan Williams

When, in the practice of Buddhist meditation, you are given a *koan* to work with, the point is to bring you to a realisation that there is no final conceptual mastery possible of the situation in which you exist, that all your perceptions are multiply conditioned rather than being 'innocent' ways of seeing things that are there: that there is no *position* you need to take. One method of working with the *koan* is simply to go on articulating the responses it generates until there is literally nothing more to say and you acknowledge that there is no resolution, no 'definitive' perspective.

It is all too easily misunderstood as a nihilistic or relativistic strategy – nothing is really there, nothing is really true or significant. Any practitioner will agree that this is a travesty. Sitting with the *koan* is a radical refusal to impose sense, even the 'sense' of saying there is no meaning or truth 'out there'. It is a painful prising open of perception, breaking free of the dualisms that constrain us (passive stuff, active mind; raw material, creative energy; problems, solutions; external stimuli, internal processing…).

And it is something like this that characterises the artists in this exhibition. Yes, they have in common an almost disturbing spareness of style that resonates with some aspects of the Buddhist world; they work with palettes of very fine gradation indeed, ranging over a narrow band, without any easy dramas. But more importantly, they work with their subjects in a profoundly *koan*-like manner. Gwen John painted an enormous number of pictures of Mere Poussepin – not just because the original idea had been that she should paint a separate picture of the mother foundress for each room of the convent, but also because, as she matured as a painter, she increasingly worked over and over again with the same subject matter: the seventeenth century nun, the corner of a working room, later on the girls kneeling in the parish church, the pictures of St Therese and her sister in childhood. In much the same way, Celia Paul revisits, again and again, her mother and her sisters and a few friends and a handful of London views. Many of the specific pictures you will see in this exhibition are in fact something like the slice of living matter that is briefly isolated under a microscope; a moment in a very

Mere Poussepin, late 1920
68.7 × 51.2 cm
Southampton City Art Gallery

prolonged process of engagement with a single subject. They are not 'definitive' statements of a vision.

This is not quite the same as what we see in a Monet, for example, a compulsion to rework subjects in different lights, at different seasons or times of day. It is a deliberate 'sitting', as the meditator would put it, with a small range of subject matter, not even differentiated by light, season or whatever, and rendering its actuality by the constant questioning of what you *think* you have just seen. It is a deliberate exhausting of ordinary seeing. The subject matter comes to be charged with unfathomable density as it is shown to generate perception after perception. As with the *koan*, it is not that this practice leads to an emptying-out of the world; it empties out the greedy and/or tidy-minded looking eye, and so allows what is there to 'unfold' more and more deeply.

In that sense, it issues in a far fuller world for the viewer/ contemplator. Even the single example, looked at in this light, invites a slow and patient engagement.

This relates to the paradox that painting which does not in the least seek for anything like photographic realism in its depiction of faces or settings has the effect of compelling a recognition of overwhelming life, of some 'form' that flashes in and around the particular moments of fixed gazing represented in any one work. And the narrow palette – both artists in fact work over their careers with a surprisingly broad variety of colour tones, but in particular works, even particular periods, restrict themselves to an ascetically disciplined sliver of the spectrum – intensifies this.

Talking about 'mysteriousness' in such a context is a bit of a cliché, too readily suggesting a portentous vagueness or a teasing reticence. It is not the word; but we need something in the same territory for an art that warns us not to suppose we have *contained* the subject matter in any one perception. The way these two artists achieve this warning is different. 'Reticence' is a word that comes to mind in looking at Gwen John, as if the artist is very clearly stepping back; the 'dusty' effect of the brushwork, a seeing as if in a strong light saturated with tiny particles, makes us very conscious of the character of the painting as a *surface*, rather as in a traditional icon, something formally quite finished, the artist having moved away, yet capturing the simple presence of one moment among others. The light itself appears almost as a veiling and so a distancing, a medium that forbids too much false intimacy or immediacy. Celia Paul allows the traces of something unfinished to mark her canvases, trails of paint, untenanted space, a certain rawness of isolation or vulnerability: and this gives to her figures more of a 'pathos' of incompletion; these are faces and figures who are made to be *aware* in and through the painting of their own painful singleness, of the poignancy of the moment worked with. Returning to the Buddhist comparison, it is as if her subjects are themselves caught up in the sitting, in the *koan* work; whereas Gwen John's images are more obviously data for the meditating observer.

To call this *meditative* painting is not simply to say that it is quiet and thoughtful – indeed some of Celia Paul's register could not be called quiet if that is taken to mean emotionally equable. The word applies in a more demanding sense: this is painting that requires concentrated response over time, steadily sifting 'readings' that are too rapid, too facile, too complacent. Meditation in religious tradition – as both these painters are well aware – demands a constant circling around the illusions of the self, a diagnostic watchfulness, a readiness to move away and begin again, aware of what has not yet been seen or said and aware that there will not be a point where everything has been seen or said. And, as we have seen, the effect is not a visual world drained or 'disenchanted' but one that ceaselessly invites any viewer who is prepared to put aside the hunger for drama and acknowledge a hunger for transparency to and for what's there. The life-*koan*, in fact, as some call it. What we see is a certain stillness; as if only in this unceasing holding and then leaving of deeply particular perceptions of the same perceived object can we encounter what steadily – timelessly if you will – holds them together *as* an object, as what is *given* to view.

Dr Rowan Williams

Archbishop of Canterbury

QUESTIONS OF AFFINITY: GWEN JOHN AND CELIA PAUL

Simon Martin

There is a particular quality of introspection, of stillness, which is present in the paintings of both Gwen John and Celia Paul. It is an uncommon quality, one that by its very nature is difficult to pin down in any definite way: an atmosphere that seems to reflect the artist's disposition, a distillation of the artist's vision. Both artists paint subtle portraits that are not definite statements of an individual's external identity, but, rather, tentative expressions of being. Their self-possessed subjects are studies of form and tone in subdued colours and scumbled paint. The construction of the spaces they inhabit endows the viewer with a sense of privileged intimacy, as if one has been allowed to share a moment of quietude with the sitter.

Yet the affinities between Gwen John and Celia Paul are not limited to formal qualities or their ability to create a sense of inner mood in their work, for there are intriguing parallels in the lives of these two women artists. Both studied at the Slade School of Fine Arts, albeit eighty years apart, both were model and muse to internationally famous male artists, and yet, both have maintained a powerfully independent strength of vision in their own painting.

Born in Wales, Gwen John (1876–39) was the sister of the artist Augustus John. After moving to Paris in 1904 she met the sculptor Auguste Rodin and began to model for him, posing as a Muse for his monument to Whistler. She became his mistress at the age of 28, more than 30 years his junior, and wrote over two thousand letters to him that are now housed at the Rodin Museum in Paris. Gwen John once wrote of how: 'A beautiful life is to be lived in the shadows, but with peace, order and tranquillity.' Her oft-quoted 'desire for a more interior life' seems to be encapsulated in her meditative painting A Corner of the Artist's Room in Paris (1907), showing a table and wicker chair in her attic studio in the Rue du Cherche Midi, where she lived from 1907 to 1909. The London studio of Celia Paul (b.1959) has a similar character: at the top of eighty stairs in an Edwardian building opposite the British Museum, its sparse rooms are similarly illuminated by diffuse light from the windows. The studio was bought for her by Lucian Freud, who had taught her in 1978 during her studies at the Slade School, and for whom she modelled in the early 1980s. Celia Paul features in several celebrated paintings by Freud such as Naked Girl with

Egg (1981), Girl in a Striped Nightshirt (1985), Painter and Model (1986–7) and Large Interior W11 (After Watteau) (1981–83). As with Gwen John, the relationship between being both artist's model and painter of portraits seems to have informed her own sensitive way of looking and capturing the sitter as a presence, and the associated vulnerabilities of this.

In 1984 Celia Paul had a child by Freud, named Frank Paul, who is also an artist. She recalls how Freud himself was conscious of Rodin and his love affairs, noting the coincidence of sharing his own birthday on 8th December with Rodin's former lover Camille Claudel, while his own former lover Suzy Boyt shared her birthday on 12th November with Rodin. Freud would speak of how he admired Gwen John's purity of intention, that she had given herself up to love for Rodin and how he felt this was a good thing, as if Celia Paul should have done the same for him. Commenting on both her own relationship with Freud, and that of John and Rodin, Paul has observed: 'If you are with another artist it can challenge your identity in a much more painful way.' Following Freud's death in 2011, Paul painted a series of fourteen canvases entitled Separation, akin to the Biblical Stations of the Cross. This series forms a mystical treatment of the pain of grief, features one painting in which the artist is presented as the Virgin Mary, with the Annunciation taking place in her bedroom, just as Gwen John had reworked Rogier van der Weyden's Annunciation (c1435) for her self-portrait Girl Reading at the Window (1911, Museum of Modern Art, New York.) Although Celia Paul is not conventionally religious, she is, in the words of William Feaver, 'a spiritual painter in that she concerns herself with the redeeming features of life, a painter bent on seeing the universal in the personal and in making the personal truthful. (John Donne's "one little room an everywhere.")' Celia Paul was brought up in a religious family: her father was Canon of Bristol Cathedral and later appointed Bishop of Bradford, and several of her paintings of her mother Pamela Paul are presentations of faith in action, with titles such as My Mother and God and Study: My Mother and the Cross. She has spoken of how, 'I remember reading in Samuel Beckett, who didn't believe, where he said that every work of art was a prayer. And it is very important to prepare myself before. To try to feel as still as I can. And then when I work, it does actually feel like a crisis. I am really calling for help.' Seated in contemplation, with her hand cupped in her lap, Pamela Paul's pose in paintings such as My Mother (2007) has an affinity with Gwen John's paintings of Mére Poussepin, the foundress of the order of the Dominican Sisters of Charity who had a convent at Meudon. After being received into the Roman Catholic Church in 1913, Gwen John had accepted a request from the nuns at the convent to make a painted copy of a portrait, and eventually painted at least six known versions each with a benign, self-contemplative aspect.

Gwen John never painted a portrait of a man, and in a letter to her friend Ursula Tyrwhitt she spoke of how: 'I think if we are to do beautiful pictures we ought to be free from family conventions and ties.' In contrast, Celia Paul has painted several portraits of her son Frank and other male sitters, but she has also repeatedly painted her mother and her four sisters, leading Lawrence Gowing to describe Pamela Paul as her Monte Sainte-Victoire. Celia Paul's watercolours of her sisters and herself make a powerful statement about the intimacy and understanding of sisterhood. They present an all-female space in which the complicated power dynamics of artist and model are subtly and profoundly altered. In the group portraits Celia's sisters sit side-by-side in unadorned gowns made by a niece, Alice Archer, their forms dissolving into translucent rivulets of paint down the paper. She has spoken of how, 'The similarities between us made me think of the fragility of identity, not just my family's but in portraiture as a whole.'

The affinity between the lives and work of Gwen John and Celia Paul is palpable and complex. Yet one would not wish to suggest some form of conscious emulation. As William Feaver has noted, Celia Paul's work is fundamentally different in that her paintings as 'more uneven, more testing perhaps, certainly more exploratory.' Yet, despite being separated by over eighty years, they share a sensibility that is expressed in the stillness and timeless quality of their paintings.

Simon Martin

Head of Collections and Exhibitions,
Pallant House Gallery

Still Life with Straw Hat, mid 1920s
27 × 33 cm
Anonymous Private Collection

Portrait of a Lady (Maud Broughton-Leigh) 1910–11
20.4 × 15.5 cm
Courtesy of Browse & Darby LTD

LIST OF OILS
Celia Paul

1. My Mother with a Rose 2006
   Oil on canvas
   81.2 × 81.2 cm / 32 × 32 in
   Private Collection

2. Post Office Tower 2010
   Oil on canvas
   25.4 × 15.2 cm / 10 × 6 in
   Private Collection

3. St George's, Bloomsbury 2010
   Oil on canvas
   25.4 × 17.8 cm / 10 × 7 in
   Private Collection

4. Juliette, Autumn 2006
   Oil on canvas
   76.2 × 76.2 cm / 30 × 30 in
   Private Collection

5. Self-Portrait, June 2010
   Oil on canvas
   25.4 × 25.4 cm /10 × 10 in

6. Jane 2003
   Oil on canvas
   46 × 46 cm / 18 1/8 × 18 1/8 in
   Private Collection

7. Margot Henderson 2003
   Oil on canvas
   46.3 × 46 cm / 18 1/4 × 18 1/8 in
   Private Collection

8. Annela 2012
   Oil on canvas
   144.8 × 106.7 cm / 57 × 42 in

9. Painter and Model 2012
   Oil on canvas
   137.2 × 76.2 cm / 54 × 30 in

1. My Mother with a Rose 2006

Oil on canvas
81.2 × 81.2 cm / 32 × 32 in

2. Post Office Tower 2010

Oil on canvas
25.4 × 15.2 cm / 10 × 6 in

3. St George's, Bloomsbury 2010

Oil on canvas
25.4 × 17.8 cm / 10 × 7 in

4. Juliette, Autumn 2006
Oil on canvas
76.2 × 76.2 cm / 30 × 30 in

5. Self-Portrait, June 2010

Oil on canvas
25.4 × 25.4 cm / 10 × 10 in

6. Jane 2003
Oil on canvas
46 × 46 cm / 18 1/8 × 18 1/8 in

7. Margot Henderson 2003
Oil on canvas
46.3 × 46 cm / 18 1/4 × 18 1/8 in

8. Annela 2012

Oil on canvas
144.8 × 106.7 cm / 57 × 42 in

9. Painter and Model 2012

Oil on canvas
137.2 × 76.2 cm / 54 × 30 in

LIST OF WATERCOLOURS
Celia Paul

10. **My Mother 2007**

 Watercolour
 105.4 × 100.3 cm / 41 1/2 × 39 1/2 in
 Private Collection

11. **My Mother and Me 2003**

 Watercolour
 137.2 × 121.9 cm / 54 × 48 in
 Private Collection

12. **Five Sisters 2010**

 Watercolour on paper mounted on canvas
 127.0 × 128.3 cm / 50 × 50 1/2 in
 Private Collection

13. **Self-Portrait 2004**

 Watercolour
 45.1 × 45.1 cm / 17 3/4 × 17 3/4 in
 Private Collection

14. **My Mother with Flowers 2004**

 Watercolour
 101 × 106.7 cm / 39 3/4 × 42 in
 Private Collection

10. My Mother 2007
Watercolour
105.4 × 100.3 cm / 41 1/2 × 39 1/2 in

11. My Mother and Me 2003
Watercolour
137.2 × 121.9 cm / 54 × 48 in

12. Five Sisters 2010
Watercolour on paper mounted on canvas
127.0 × 128.3 cm / 50 × 50 1/2 in

13. Self-Portrait 2004
Watercolour
45.1 × 45.1 cm / 17 3/4 × 17 3/4 in

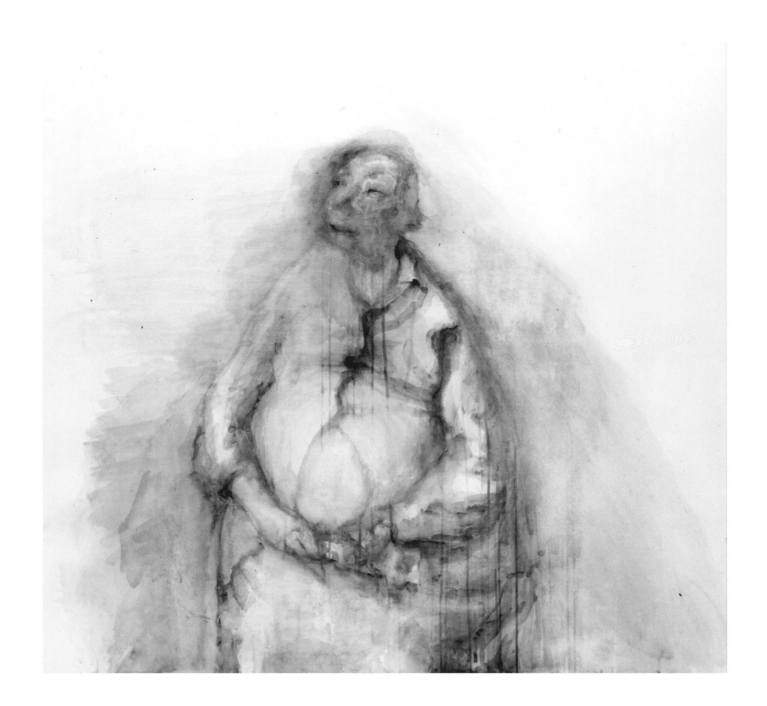

14. My Mother with Flowers 2004
Watercolour
101 × 106.7 cm / 39 3/4 × 42 in

LIST OF PRINTS
Celia Paul

15. My Mother and the Sea 1999

Soft ground etching
Plate 29.2 × 21.5 cm
Sheet 56.8 × 37.8 cm

16. Kate Pregnant 1996

Soft-ground etching
Plate 35.2 × 29.2 cm
Sheet 65.7 × 52.4 cm

17. Kate and Molly 2002

Soft ground etching
Plate 7.5 × 11.2 cm
Sheet 25 × 27.6 cm

18. Little Self-Portrait 1 2002

Soft ground etching
Plate 7 × 7 cm
Sheet 28.6 × 22.7 cm

19. Lucy 2001

Soft ground etching
Plate 14.7 × 12.1 cm
Sheet 33.1 × 26.6 cm

20. My Mother with Mandy 2005

Soft ground etching
Plate 14.5 × 16.8 cm

21. Molly 2005

Soft ground etching
Plate 6.5 × 5.3 cm
Sheet 22.5 × 18.5 cm

22. Figure Approaching the British Museum 2008

Soft ground etching
Plate 10.5 × 7.0 cm
Sheet 30.5 × 20.5 cm

23. Room 2008

Soft ground etching
Plate 11.5 × 15 cm
Sheet 34.5 × 35.5 cm

Printed by Dorothea Wight at Studio Prints.

24. Lucian Sleeping 1987

Charcoal
19 1/4 × 16 1/8 in

25. Frank 1997

Charcoal
9 × 6 in

15. My Mother and the Sea 1999

Soft ground etching
Plate 29.2 × 21.5 cm
Sheet 56.8 × 37.8 cm

16. Kate Pregnant 1996

Soft-ground etching
Plate 35.2 × 29.2 cm
Sheet 65.7 × 52.4 cm

17. Kate and Molly 2002

Soft ground etching
Plate 7.5 × 11.2 cm
Sheet 25 × 27.6 cm

19. Lucy 2001

Soft ground etching
Plate 14.7 × 12.1 cm
Sheet 33.1 × 26.6 cm

18. Little Self-Portrait 1 2002

Soft ground etching
Plate 7 × 7 cm
Sheet 28.6 × 22.7 cm

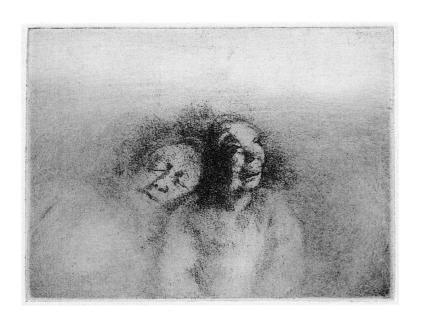

20. My Mother with Mandy 2005

Soft ground etching
Plate 14.5 × 16.8 cm

21. Molly 2005

Soft ground etching
Plate 6.5 × 5.3 cm
Sheet 22.5 × 18.5 cm

22. Figure Approaching the British Museum 2008

Soft ground etching
Plate 10.5 × 7.0 cm
Sheet 30.5 × 20.5 cm

23. Room 2008

Soft ground etching
Plate 11.5 × 15 cm
Sheet 34.5 × 35.5 cm

24. Lucian Sleeping 1987

Charcoal
19 1/4 × 16 1/8 in

25. Frank 1997

Charcoal
9 × 6 in

SEPARATION
Celia Paul

Recently I've been inclined to look at the early (mostly Italian) paintings in the Sainsbury Wing of the National Gallery. The aura of stillness is particularly powerful in these rooms. The theme is predominantly religious with the greatest number of paintings depicting the Madonna and Child. I began to think about Mary and her feelings.

There are two contrasting small paintings in the National Gallery: The Virgin and Child in an Interior by School of Robert Campin and Crucifixion by Antonello. There can be no more intimate image of closeness than the interior: mother and son sitting in the warm light of the fire, cradled in each other's arms so that they form a perfect entity. In the crucifixion the figures of the Virgin and St John are separated from their beloved Christ by an impossibly tall cross. There can be no more desolate and powerful representation of the final separateness of death than this.

I think the theme of Separation has been subtly present in my work all along but I suddenly felt driven to express it in a more explicit way. These are the only images I have painted from my imagination rather than from life, and the nearest thing to expressionist paintings I've ever done. There are 14 because I wanted them to be a sort of Stations of the Cross. They vary greatly in size according to whether the image is intimate or dramatic.

The title of the series is 'Separation'.

LIST OF 'SEPARATION' PAINTINGS 2011
Celia Paul

26. The Virgin
Oil on canvas
10 × 12 in

27. The Annunciation
Oil on canvas
22 × 20 in

28. Madonna and Child
Oil on canvas
50 × 50 in

29. Separation
Oil on canvas
30 × 20 in

30. The Madonna Separate
Oil on canvas
22 × 20 in

31. Waiting
Oil on canvas
22 × 20 in

32. At the Base of the Cross
Oil on canvas
22 × 20 in

33. Crucifixion
Oil on canvas
18 × 10 in

34. Pieta
Oil on canvas
56 × 56 in

35. Dark Night
Oil on canvas
22 × 16 in

36. How it is
Oil on canvas
22 × 20 in

37. Mary
Oil on canvas
10 × 12 in

38. The Assumption
Oil on canvas
50 × 50 in

39. Tree
Oil on canvas
56 × 56 in

26. The Virgin
Oil on canvas
10 × 12 in

27. The Annunciation
Oil on canvas
22 × 20 in

28. Madonna and Child

Oil on canvas
50 × 50 in

29. Separation

Oil on canvas
30 × 20 in

30. The Madonna Separate

Oil on canvas

22 × 20 in

31. Waiting

Oil on canvas
22 × 20 in

32. At the Base of the Cross
Oil on canvas
22 × 20 in

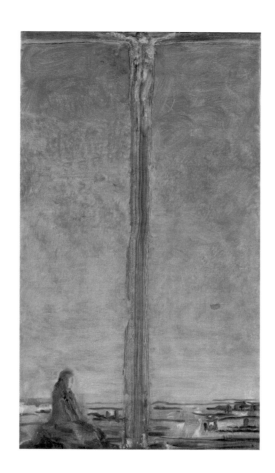

33. Crucifixion

Oil on canvas
18 × 10 in

34. Pieta

Oil on canvas
56 × 56 in

35. Dark Night
Oil on canvas
22 × 16 in

36. How it is
Oil on canvas
22 × 20 in

37. Mary
Oil on canvas
10 × 12 in

38. The Assumption

Oil on canvas
50 × 50 in

39. Tree
Oil on canvas
56 × 56 in

BIOGRAPHIES

Gwendolen Mary John

1876	Born 22 June Haverfordwest, Wales
1895–98	Attended Slade School of Art with brother Augustus John
1900	Exhibited for the first time at the New English Art Club
1903	Exhibited with Augustus John at Carfax and Company
1904	Moved to Paris where she met and fell in love with Auguste Rodin
1910	Moved to Meudon, Paris where she remained for the rest of her life
1913	Converted to Catholicism
1919	Exhibited in Paris for the first time at the Salon d'Automne where she exhibited regularly until the mid 1920s
1939	Died 18 September in Dieppe, France

Celia Paul

1959	Born in Trivandrum, India, 11 November
1976–81	Studied at the Slade School of Art
1986	First solo exhibition at Bernard Jacobson gallery
1991	Regular solo exhibitions at Marlborough Fine Art since 1991
2004	Retrospective exhibition at Abbot Hall,
2011	First prize for the Ruth Borchard Self-Portrait award

One son by Lucian Freud, Frank Paul, born December 10th 1984

Lives and works in London.

MARLBOROUGH

London
Marlborough Fine Art (London) Ltd
6 Albemarle Street
London, W1S 4BY
Telephone: +44-(0)20-7629 5161
Telefax: +44-(0)20-7629 6338
mfa@marlboroughfineart.com
info@marlboroughgraphics.com
www.marlboroughfineart.com

New York
Marlborough Gallery Inc.
40 West 57th Street
New York, N.Y. 10019
Telephone: +1-212-541 4900
Telefax: +1-212-541 4948
mny@marlboroughgallery.com
www.marlboroughgallery.com

Chelsea
Marlborough Chelsea
545 West 25th Street
New York, N.Y. 10001
Telephone: +1-212-463 8634
Telefax: +1-212-463 9658
chelsea@marlboroughgallery.com

Monte Carlo
Marlborough Monaco
4 Quai Antoine Ier
MC 98000
Monaco
Telephone: +377-9770 2550
Telefax: +377-9770 2559
art@marlborough-monaco.com
www.marlborough-monaco.com

Madrid
Galería Marlborough SA
Orfila 5
28010 Madrid
Telephone: +34-91-319 1414
Telefax: +34-91-308 4345
info@galeriamarlborough.com
www.galeriamarlborough.com

Santiago
Galería A.M.S. Marlborough
Avenida Nueva Costanera 3723
Vitacura, Santiago, Chile
Telephone: +56-2-799 3180
Telefax: +56-2-799 3181
info@amsgaleria.cl
www.amsgaleria.cl

Barcelona
Marlborough Barcelona
Valencia, 284, 1r 2a A
Barcelona, 08007
Telephone: +34-93-467 4454
Telefax: +34-93-467 4451
infobarcelona@galeriamarlborough.com

London
Agents for
Frank Auerbach
Stephen Conroy
Christopher Couch
John Davies
David Dawson
Daniel Enkaoua
Karl Gerstner
Catherine Goodman
Daniela Gullotta
Dieter Hacker
Maggi Hambling
Clive Head
Paul Hodgson
John Hubbard
Allen Jones
Nina Murdoch
Hughie O'Donoghue
Thérèse Oulton
Celia Paul
Cathie Pilkington
Paula Rego
Joe Tilson
John Virtue
The Estate of Avigdor Arikha
The Estate of Steven Campbell

The Estate of Matthew Carr
The Estate of Chen Yifei
The Estate of Ken Kiff
The Estate of Oskar Kokoschka
The Estate of Raymond Mason
The Estate of Victor Pasmore
The Estate of Sarah Raphael
The Estate of Euan Uglow
The Estate of Victor Willing

Important works available by
Impressionists and Post-Impressionists
Twentieth Century European Masters
German Expressionists
Post War American Artists

Modern Masters Prints,
Contemporary Publications
and Photographs available from
Marlborough Graphics,
London and New York

Monte Carlo
Agents for
Roberto Barni
Davide Benati
The Estate of Alberto Magnelli

New York
Agents for
Magdalena Abakanowicz
L.C. Armstrong
Chakaia Booker
Fernando Botero
Grisha Bruskin
Dale Chihuly
Chu Teh-Chun
Vincent Desiderio
Thierry W Despont
Richard Estes
Juan Genovés
Red Grooms
Stephen Hannock
Israel Hershberg
Bill Jacklin

Kcho
Julio Larraz
Ricardo Maffei
Rashaad Newsome
Michele Oka Doner
Tom Otterness
Beverly Pepper
Arnaldo Pomodoro
Bruce Robbins
Tomás Sánchez
Steven Siegel
Hunt Slonem
Clive Smith
Kenneth Snelson
Manolo Valdés
Doug Wada
Robert Weingarten
Zao Wou-Ki
The Estate of Claudio Bravo
The Estate of R.B. Kitaj
The Estate of Jacques Lipchitz
The Estate of Clement Meadmore
The Estate of George Rickey

Madrid
Agents for
Alfonso Albacete
Juan José Aquerreta
Martín Chirino
Rafael Cidoncha
Alberto Corazón
Juan Correa
Carlos Franco
Manuel Franquelo
Juan Genovés
Luis Gordillo
Abraham Lacalle
Francisco Leiro
Antonio López García
Blanca Muñoz
Juan Navarro Baldeweg
Pelayo Ortega
David Rodríguez Caballero
Sergio Sanz
The Estate of Lucio Muñoz